Dedications

This book is dedicated to everyone that has stood by me and supported me in my quest to play drums for a living.

My wonderful girlfriend Sam Priest and my parents, Dave and Julie for their continued help and support.

My friends for life, Ben, Phil, Billy, Andy, Rob, Paul and Dan for being there and putting up with me being a poor musician.

Fellow teachers, Richard Davey, David Driver, Mike Small, Mike Fox, Lee McCrumlish and Simon Mellish for being part of our drum network and for giving me feedback on this book from the start.

The Drumsense leaders, Colin Woolway and Nick Cole, for all your help and advice and for deciding to use this book as part of the Drumsense programme.

Haydn Callow for being such a good teacher and for teaching me all this stuff in the first place.

Contact details

For information on one.8.e studio or to order further copies of this book contact Dave Hazlewood.
Tel: +44 (0)1892 750157
Email: dave@one8e.co.uk
Web: www.one8e.co.uk

For information on the Drumsense teaching programme contact Drumsense.
Tel: +44 (0)2082 880863
Email: info@drumsense.com
Web: www.drumsense.com

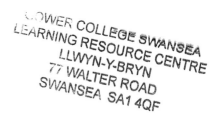

Introduction

Why learn to read drum music?

Many drummers avoid learning to read music because they don't see any benefits.

When playing in a band, either creating original songs or playing cover versions, they are not likely to be in a situation where they are given a sheet of music to read.

This may well be the case, but is that what reading music is all about?

Many years ago I didn't believe that I needed to know how to read music. It was not until I decided to take my drumming more seriously and play professionally that I realised you can't play a lot of things on the drum kit without first understanding what it is that you are playing.

I went to a drum school to develop my playing, where I had lessons on reading music, and was amazed at how logical and easy it was to learn. Obviously nothing can be achieved without practice and a bit of effort, but with a structured approach to learning a whole new world is opened up.

So what are the benefits?

The main benefit you will gain from being able to read music is faster development as a drummer. Through a greater understanding of note values and their relationship to each other, your playing will improve generally, as will your ability to learn from books and magazine articles.

You will find learning songs so much easier and quicker, because you can write down grooves or fills in notation to help practice and learn them. Also when writing songs, you will be able to write down good ideas, so that you can develop them further in your own time, (also giving the added bonus of not forgetting that essential groove between band practices).

This book covers a lot, but not everything to do with reading music. It is a great place to start, even if you know a little already, but remember there's always more out there to learn.

I had a great teacher to take me through this process, so I would recommend if possible you do the same.
Have fun,
Dave

D R U M S E N S E

Music Reading for Drummers

by

DAVE HAZLEWOOD

An introduction to reading and understanding
drum notation and basic note values

Edited by Rob Woodcock

Drumsense Publications
68-70 London Road, Croydon CR0 2TB
United Kingdom
www.drumsense.com

ISBN 978-0-9555593-1-0

DRUMSENSE - Music Reading for Drummers
This Volume: 1st edition
© Copyright 2007 David Hazlewood

Produced by one.8.e studio
Published by Drumsense Publications

Printed in England by Caligraving Ltd., Thetford, Norfolk

Edited by Rob Woodcock
Cover design by Ian Hayter

Contents

Note

In writing this book, I have not given the note values their classical names, but instead have used a more modern approach and used names based around fractions.

This approach is a lot more common now and in a lot of places has become the standard way to refer to note values.

I like to teach this way because it makes the whole process a lot more logical and easier to understand and learn.

To clarify, here is a list of the modern note names used in this book with their classical names next to them.

Whole note -------- Semi-breve

Half note --------- Minim

Quarter note ------- Crotchet

Eighth note -------- Quaver

Sixteenth note ----- Semi-quaver

When you have worked through the book and you understand everything fully, it is important to learn the classical names as well. Although you don't need to know them to work through this book and understand note values, the classical names are still used and you need to know what they are when you come across them.

Refer back to this page when you have completed the book.

It is also worth noting that the key used in this book for which drum is on which line of the stave, is the most commonly used key. You may however come across variations in some tuition books. There has never been a universal standard key used worldwide, but the key I have used has been the standard for most drummers and authors for some time now.

Kit recognition

The picture above is of a standard 5 piece drum kit.

A drum kit is made up of drums and cymbals.

5 piece refers to the number of drums only and does not include cymbals or stands.

In a standard 5 piece drum kit there is a bass drum, a snare drum and 3 tom toms (normally just called toms and are sometimes referred to as 1st, 2nd and floor toms.

The cymbals shown here include a pair of hi-hats, a ride cymbal and 2 crash cymbals.

The other bits (not labelled) that make up the drum kit are the bass drum pedal, the hi-hat stand and two cymbal stands. There will also be a drum stool to sit on.

Drum kit basic notation

Drum music is written on a **'stave'**.

Where a note is situated on the stave tells us which drum or cymbal to hit.

Here are a few pointers to help you remember them all.

1/ A cross written on the stave lets you know that you need to hit something metal (i.e. cymbals) and not a drum.

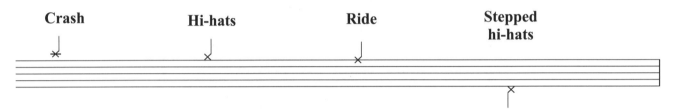

NOTE: The higher up the stave, the higher up the drum kit.

2/ A dot lets you know to play a drum.

We will begin with the notes that we will use the most.
These are the snare, bass and hi-hats.

Below is an example of how a drum groove is written. Drum kit notation is often written as if there are two instruments - one being the drums and the other the cymbals. In the example below, you can see the hi-hats are written together as one instrument, and the snare and bass are also written as one.

Music is divided into 'bars'. The example above is one bar long.

If you compare the rules of reading music to those of reading words, there are a few similarities.
Notes are the musical equivalent of letters, bars are the musical equivalent of words, while songs or charts are the musical equivalent of stories. Reading music is a lot simpler than reading words, but there is a small amount of maths involved, which we will look at a bit later on.

Basic notation exercise

1/ With this first exercise, write in the names of each drum or cymbal above the stave (as in the first bar) and then play the exercise through slowly.

Write snare, bass, high (tom), mid (tom), low (tom), hats, crash, ride, step (hi-hats).

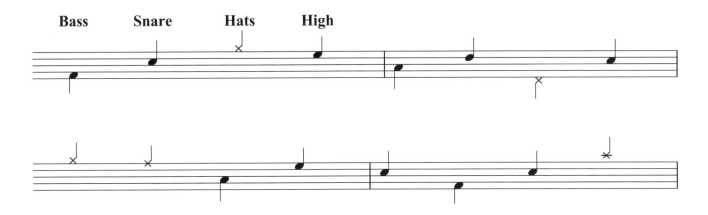

2/ In this exercise, write in just the initials for each drum or cymbal and then play the exercise through slowly.

Write - S = snare, B = bass, H = high tom, M = mid tom, L = low tom, HH = hi-hats, C = crash, R = ride, SH = stepped hi-hats.

3/ Now play this last exercise without writing any names at all.

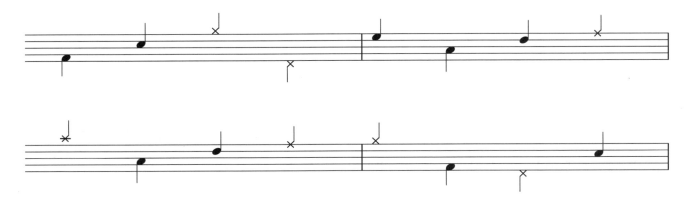

Counting and playing quarter notes

In this exercise, you will learn basic concepts that will help you throughout the rest of the book.

The first bar below has four 'quarter notes' (numbered 1 - 2 - 3 - 4) all on the snare drum line.

The second bar contains 'quarter note rests'.

To play the following and subsequent exercise, you need to remember a few things.

1/ Count 1 - 2 - 3 - 4 out loud at a slow, steady pace.

2/ Tap your foot in time with your counting throughout the exercise.

3/ When there is a 'quarter note' under a number, you play a snare drum.

4/ When there is a 'quarter note rest' under a number, you DON'T play anything.

If possible play to a click (metronome) to make sure that you are playing at a steady tempo (speed).
This will not only develop your reading skills, but will also help improve your timing.

Quarter note exercise

Now see if you can play the following exercise without the count written above the stave.
Play each line separately and then play as one piece.

Basic chart markings

To play the exercises in this book, you need to understand a few basic markings. Markings on a piece of music or exercise give you a bit more information about what you are playing and may give you extra instructions.

Here are a few of the most common markings.

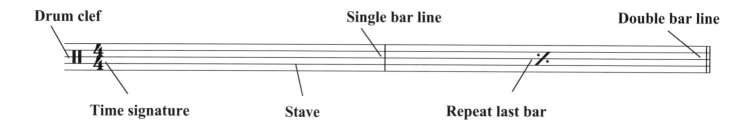

Drum clef - Tells you that the piece of music or exercise is written for drums.

Single bar line - Divides all bars throughout the piece or exercise.

Double bar lines - Signifies the end of a section (e.g. the end of a verse) within a song, but not the end of the piece.

Time signature - This tells you the size of the bars. 4/4 means 4 quarter notes in a bar. There are other time signatures, but this is the only time signature we will be using at the moment. 4/4 time is sometimes written as 'C' for 'common time' as it is the most common time signature.

Stave - The 5 lines that all music is written on.

Repeat last bar - Play exactly what you played in the previous bar.

Here are some more markings you may see.

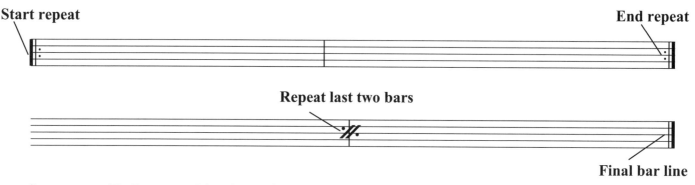

Start repeat/End repeat - Play the section between the repeat signs again.

Repeat last two bars - Play the previous two bars again.

Final bar line - End of the piece or exercise.

Chart markings exercise

1/ Play this exercise through taking care to watch for the repeat section.

2/ In this exercise make sure your counting is strong to avoid missing any bars out.

Introduction to note values

Now you have got used to counting and playing quarter notes, it s time to look at some other notes. These are called whole notes and half notes . There is just a little bit of simple maths involved to understand the relationship between these notes.

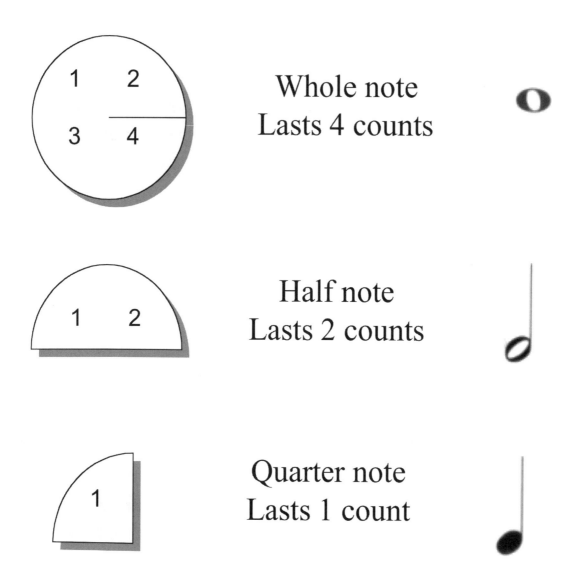

Whole note
Lasts 4 counts

Half note
Lasts 2 counts

Quarter note
Lasts 1 count

When talking about a note lasting for several counts you have to imagine the note being held as if you were blowing a trumpet. With a trumpet, the longer you blow, the longer the note lasts. With a drum there is no way to make a note last any longer than one hit. We therefore are not actually holding the note or making it last, but merely waiting until we reach the next note.

Whole, half and quarter notes

Whole notes
4 counts

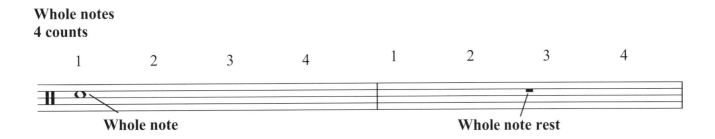

Whole note   **Whole note rest**

The note written on the snare drum line in the first bar of the stave above is a 'whole note'.
To play a whole note, hit on count '1' and hold it (wait) for counts '2', '3' and '4'.

The block hanging from the second line down in the second bar is a 'whole note rest'.
If you see a whole note rest, DON'T play anything for 4 counts.

Half notes
2 counts

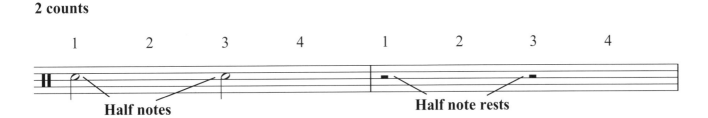

Half notes   **Half note rests**

The notes written on the snare drum line in the first bar of the stave above are 'half notes'.
To play a half note, hit on whichever number it appears and hold it (wait) for the next count.
e.g. play on count '1' and hold it (wait) for count '2'.

The blocks sitting on the third line down in the second bar are 'half note rests'.
If you see a half note rest, DON'T play for 2 counts.

Quarter notes
1 count

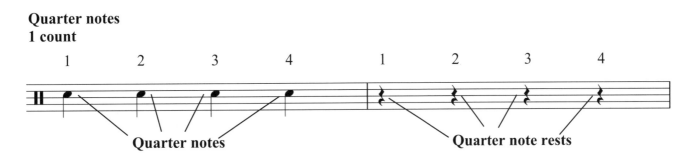

Quarter notes   **Quarter note rests**

The notes written on the snare drum line in the first bar of the stave above are 'quarter notes'.
To play a quarter note, only hit on the count that it appears.

The wavy lines in the second bar are 'quarter note rests'.
If you see a quarter note rest, DON'T play for 1 count.

Whole, half and quarter note exercise 1

Here are some exercises combining whole, half and quarter notes with their respective rests.

Remember to keep counting out loud and play slowly to start.

Play each line separately and then play as one piece.

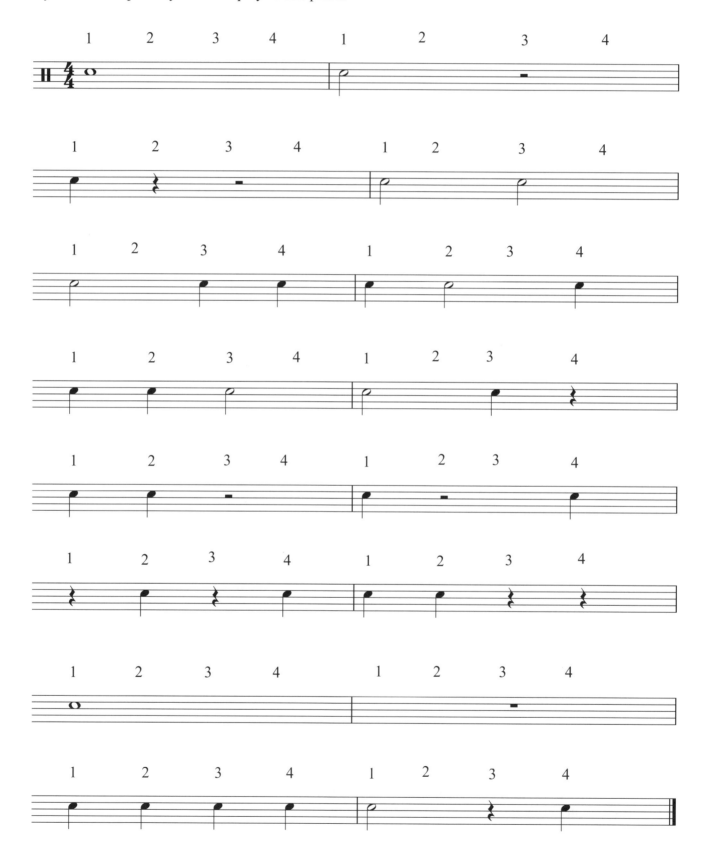

Whole, half and quarter note exercise 2

Now see if you can play the same exercise without the counting written above the stave.

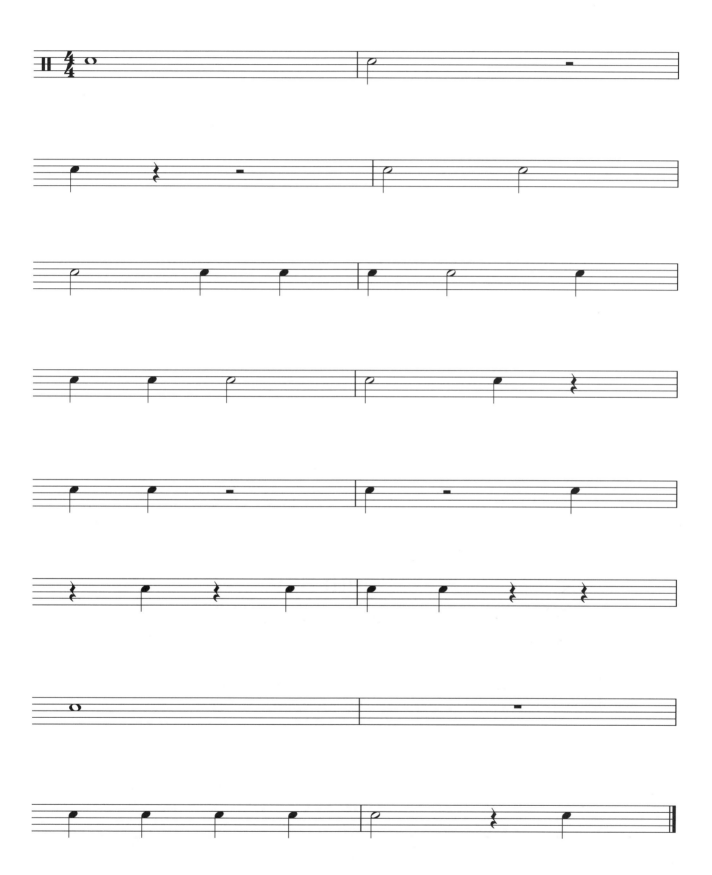

Introducing eighth notes

We are now going to look at the next note values which are eighth notes.
This is how they fit in with the notes we have already used.

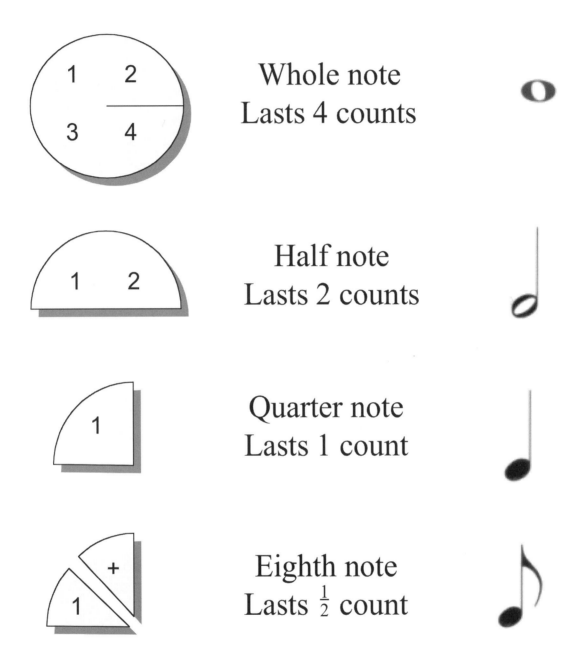

Whole note
Lasts 4 counts

Half note
Lasts 2 counts

Quarter note
Lasts 1 count

Eighth note
Lasts $\frac{1}{2}$ count

Note: An individual eighth note has a tail coming from the stem. When eighth notes are joined together the tails are joined to make a connecting line (see next page).

When playing eighth notes, you will see that there are now more notes than counts, (8 notes and only 4 counts). This is where the counting gets a little bit more confusing.

Whole note
4 counts

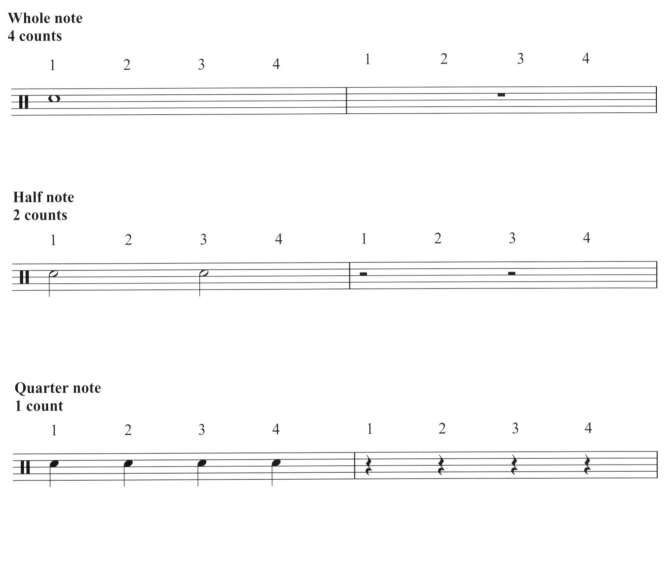

Half note
2 counts

Quarter note
1 count

Eighth note
1/2 count

Eighth notes   Eighth note rests

By looking at the count above the eighth notes, you can see that there is a note on each of the counts (1, 2, 3 and 4) and also a note in between each count shown above the stave by a '+' sign (said as 'and'). When counting out loud, you now say '1 and 2 and 3 and 4 and'.

Eighth note exercise 1

Here are some exercises using eighth notes and quarter notes.
Play each line separately and then play as one piece.

This part of the exercise combines all we have covered so far.

Eighth note exercise 2

Now play this exercise without the counting written above the stave.
Play each line separately and then play as one piece.
Remember to count out loud and use a click if possible

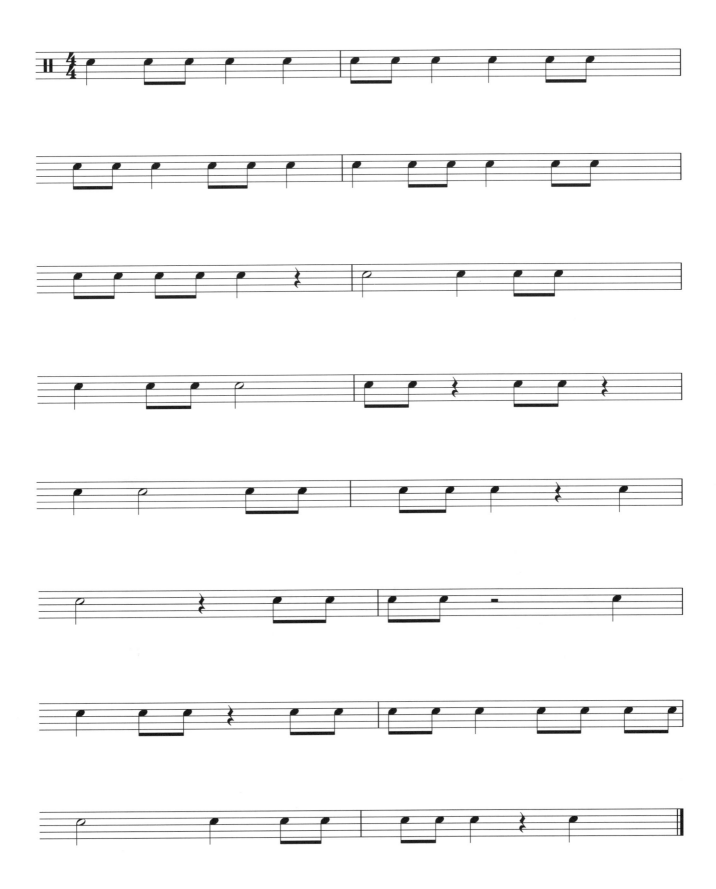

15

Introducing sixteenth notes

Here are all the note values we've covered so far as well as the next notes to look at, which are sixteenth notes.

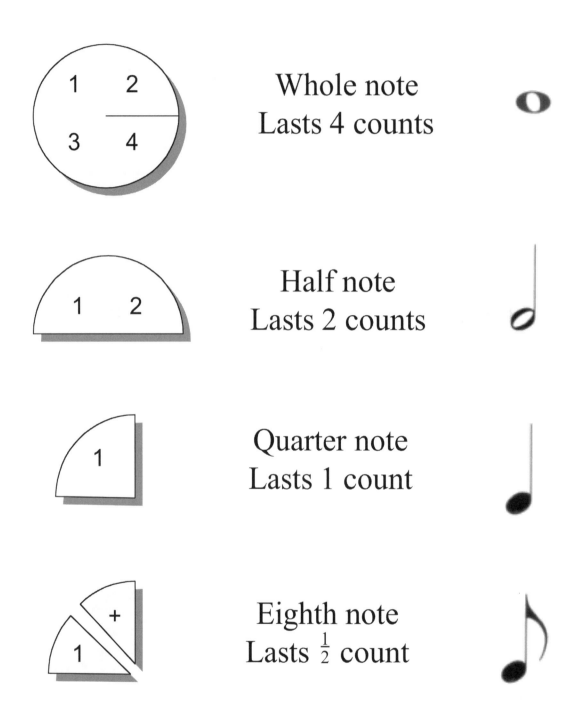

Whole note
Lasts 4 counts

Half note
Lasts 2 counts

Quarter note
Lasts 1 count

Eighth note
Lasts $\frac{1}{2}$ count

Sixteenth note
Lasts $\frac{1}{4}$ count

Note: Sixteenth notes have 2 tails. When 4 sixteenth notes are put together, their tails are joined making 2 lines (see next page).

You can now see that by using basic fractions, you can work out and remember the values of each of the notes quite easily.

All note values relate back to the whole note.

- There are 2 half notes to a whole note.
- There are 4 quarter notes to a whole note.
- There are 8 eighth notes to a whole note.
- There are 16 sixteenth notes to a whole note.

When playing in 4/4 time these numbers fit into a bar in the same way.

- There are 2 half notes in a bar.
- There are 4 quarter notes in a bar.
- There are 8 eighth notes in a bar.
- There are 16 sixteenth notes in a bar.

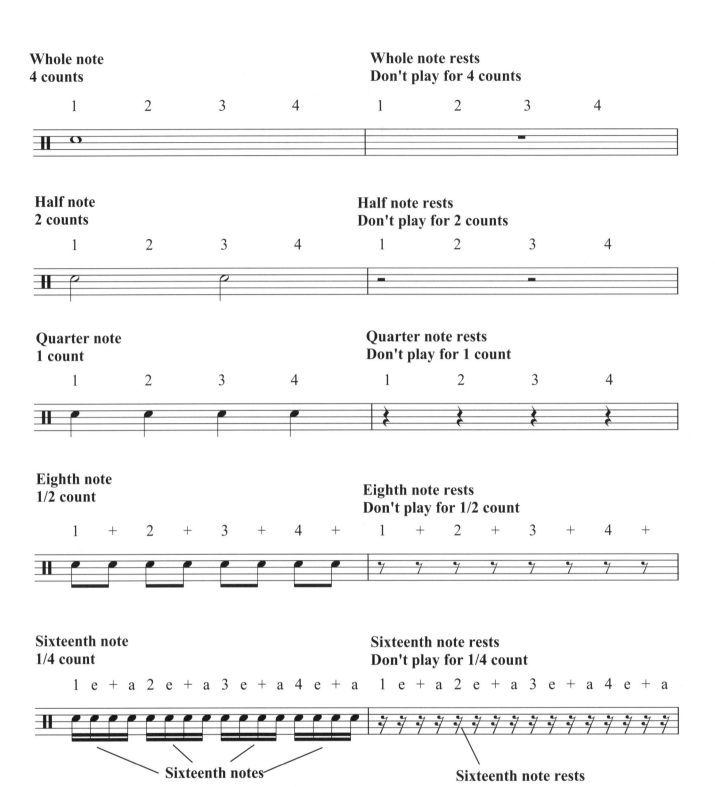

As with eighth notes, there are now even more notes and still only 4 counts.

The sixteenths are grouped in lots of four and the first one of each group falls on the 1, the 2, the 3 and the 4.
The third sixteenth in each group falls on the '+' .
The other sixteenths are between these.

The counting therefore now becomes 1 e + a,   2 e + a,   3 e + a,   4 e + a.
(said '1 e and a, 2 e and a, 3 e and a, 4 e and a')

Timing exercise

This exercise is designed to help you play each of the different note values at a constant tempo and understand their relationship to each other when playing in time.

Play each line once and then move onto the next.
When you get to the bottom of the exercise, work your way back up to the top again.
Repeat several times.

Play to a click, starting slowly at first, but experiment at different tempos.
When you find the exercise easy, mix it up by playing the different lines in a random order.

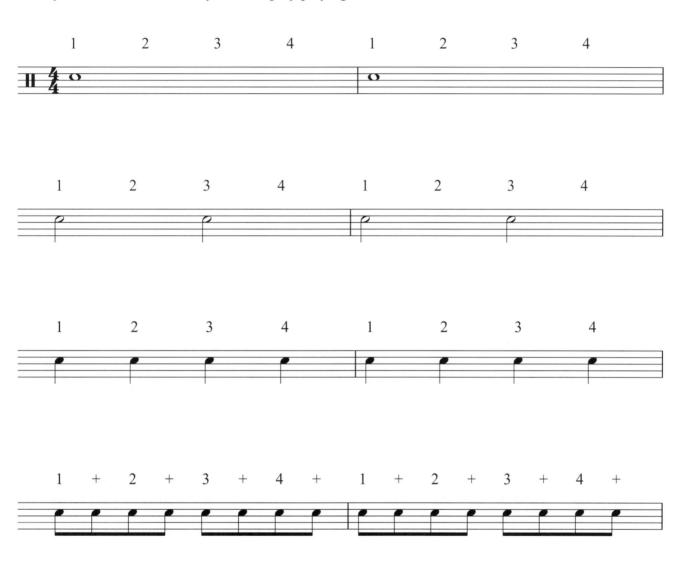

Sixteenth note exercise 1

Here is an exercise using sixteenth notes with eighth and quarter notes.
Play each line separately and then play as one piece.

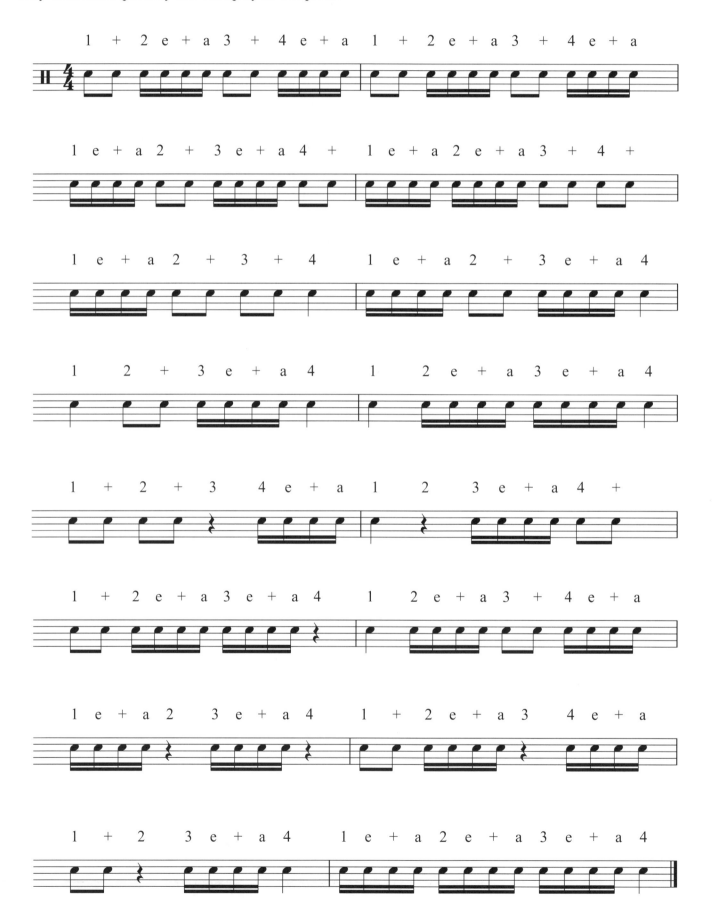

Sixteenth note exercise 2

Now see if you can play the same exercise without the count written above the stave.

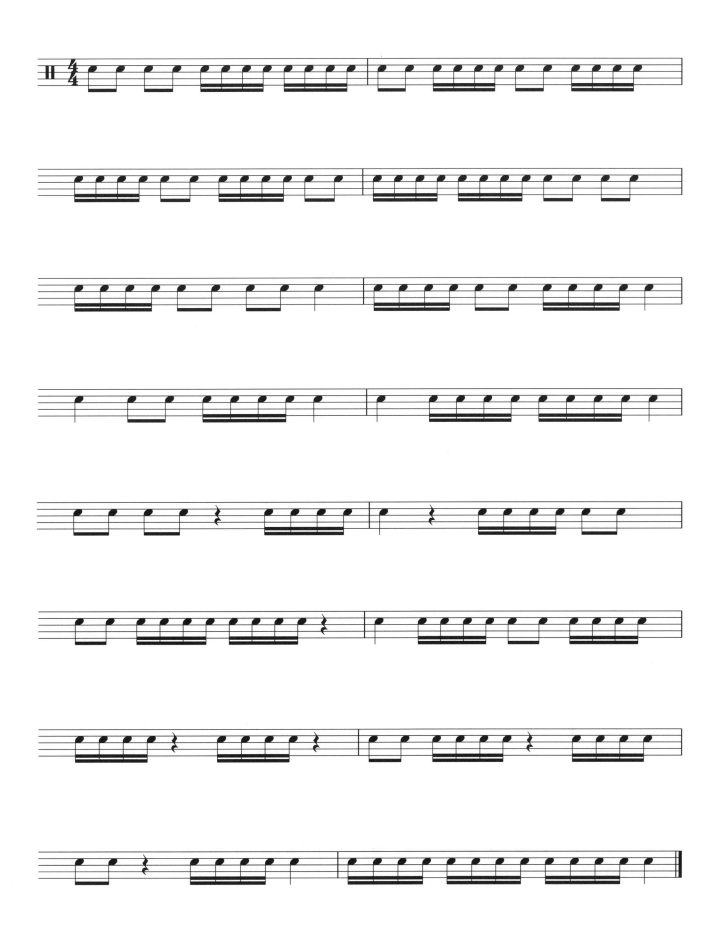

Combined exercise 1

These exercises combine everything covered so far.

Combined exercise 2

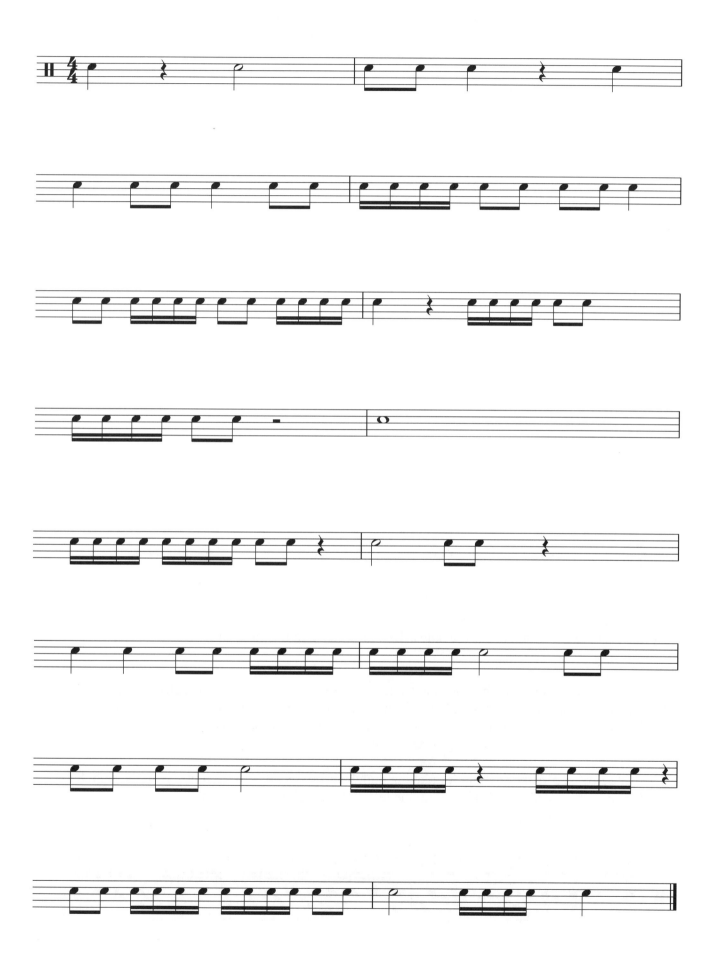

Introducing triplets

Everything we have looked at so far has been what is known as 'straight meter', meaning that the notes have a straight and even feel to them. Going from playing quarter notes to eighth notes to sixteenth notes is fairly easy as you are just doubling the amount of beats each time.

Triplets are slightly different and can therefore be a bit more difficult to play.

The word 'Triplet' simply means '3 in the space of 2'.

What this means is that where you have 2 notes in straight meter there will be 3 in its equivalent triplet. All notes have an equivalent triplet, so you can have 'half note triplets', 'quarter note triplets', 'eighth note triplets' and 'sixteenth note triplets'.
This may sound confusing, but we will only be looking at eighth and sixteenth note triplets in this book as these are the most common.

Let's start by looking at 'eighth note triplets'.

The top bar below contains normal eighth notes, while the bar below it contains eighth note triplets. Notice that for every two eighth notes there are three eighth note triplets.

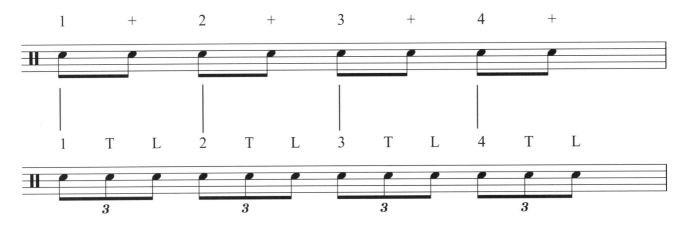

The counting for eighth note triplets is '1 - Trip - Let, 2 - Trip - Let, 3 Trip - Let, 4 Trip - Let. (Written as 1 T L, 2 T L, 3 T L, 4 T L).
Notice also the '3' written under the notes. This indicates that they are triplets.

One thing to watch out for when playing triplets is the 'sticking'. Sticking basically means which hand plays which beat. Alternating hands is the best way to play at the moment. This is easy with eight notes and sixteenth notes as you can start with your lead (strongest) hand and it will always be on the pulse (the pulse is where you are tapping your foot on the quarter note).

The bar below shows the sticking for playing eighth and sixteenth notes leading with the right hand (if you are left handed, play leading with the left). I have written in a bass drum to show where the quarter note pulse is.

Notice now that when playing eighth note triplets you can start with your lead hand but, your lead hand won't be on the pulse all the way through the bar. Again I have written in the bass drum to show where the pulse is.

R L R L R L R L R L R L   R L R L R L R L R L R L

Play the exercise below to get used to counting and playing eighth note triplets.

I have written the count above the stave and the sticking below the stave.

1 T L 2 T L 3 T L 4 T L   1 T L 2 T L 3 T L 4 T L

R L R L R L R L R L R L   R L R L R L R L R L R L

Play the next exercise and repeat to get used to mixing eighth note triplets and quarter notes.

1   2 T L 3   4 T L 1   2 T L 3   4 T L

R   L R L R   L R L R   L R L R   L R L

This is a similar exercise to the last, but starts with the eighth note triplets.

1 T L 2   3 T L 4   1 T L 2   3 T L 4

R L R L   R L R L   R L R L   R L R L

Eighth note triplet exercise 1

This first exercise combines eighth note triplets with quarter notes.

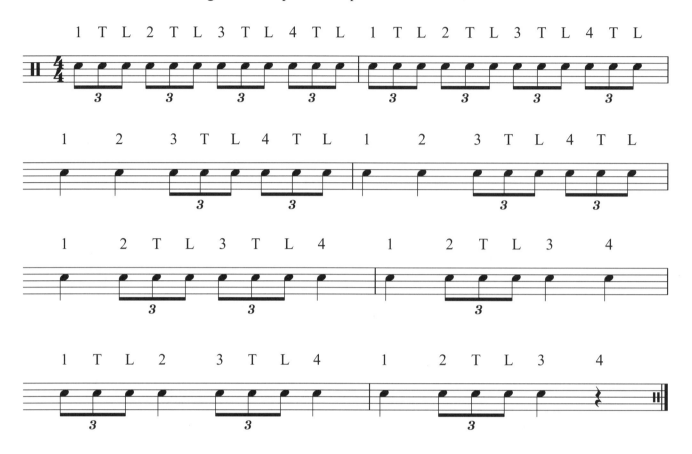

This part of the exercise includes eighth notes which will give a slightly odd feel.
Remember to count out loud as this will really help now.

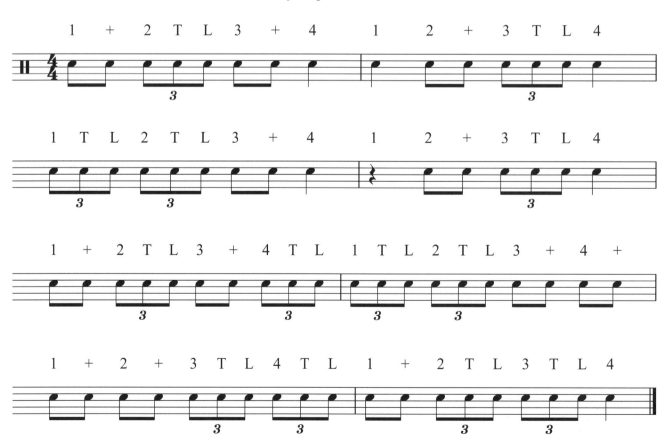

Eighth note triplet exercise 2

This exercise combines quarter notes and eighth note triplets.
Play each line separately and then play as one piece.

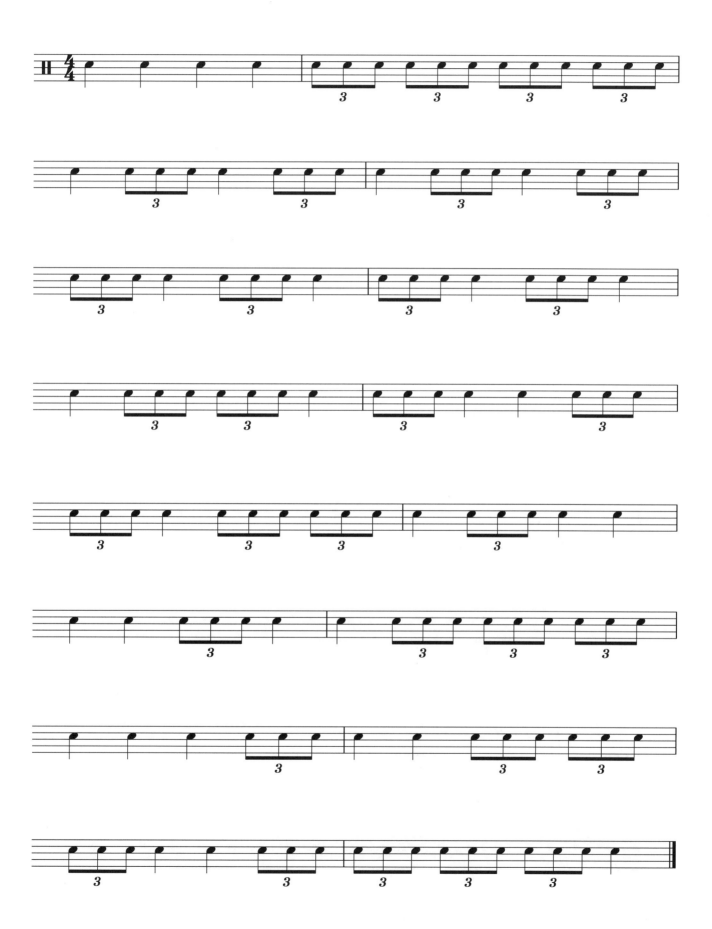

Eighth note triplet exercise 3

This exercise combines quarter notes, eighth notes and eighth note triplets.
Play each line separately and then play as one piece.

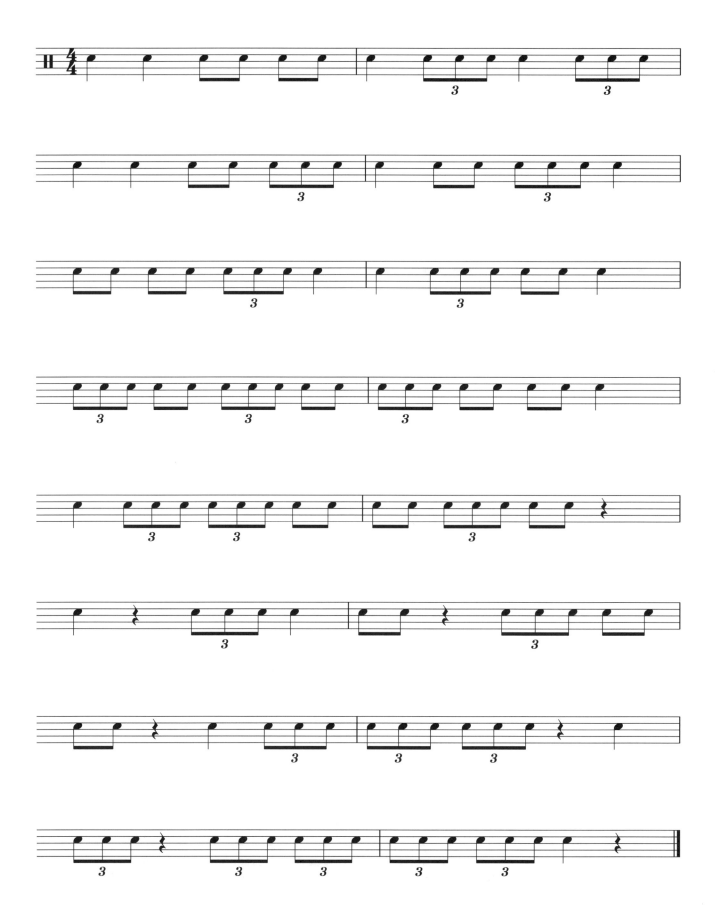

Sixteenth note triplets

The last group of notes to look at in this book is 'sixteenth note triplets'.

Sixteenth note triplets are the triplet version of sixteenth notes.
For every two sixteenth notes there are three sixteenth note triplets.

As you can see in the two bars below, the Sixteenth notes are grouped into groups of four and so the sixteenth notes triplets are grouped into groups of six.

Notice how the sixteenth note triplets have '3' written above them to show that they are triplets.

Sixteenth note triplets are a bit harder to count, as there are a lot of notes. Even at slow tempos, sixteenth note triplets may seem a bit too quick to count all of them.

Below are some ideas for counting sixteenth note triplets. The first two ideas are good because they give you the '+' which falls in the same place as the '+' when counting eighth and sixteenth notes. This will help with timing as well as giving you a good feel for the triplets

1/ Count '1 - trip - let - and - trip - let'

2/ Count '1 - e - a - and - e - a'

3/ Sixteenth note triplets are sometimes called 'sextuplets'. They also sometimes have a '6' above the notes rather than two '3's. This is how I have written this last example for counting.
In this example, you just count all of the notes in each group '1 - 2 - 3 - 4 - 5 - 6'.

Experiment counting using the different examples above and then use the one that you find easiest.

Sixteenth note triplet exercise 1

In these sixteenth note triplet exercises I have not written in a count above the stave so that you can use the counting system you feel most comfortable with.

The following exercises combine quarter notes, eighth notes, eighth note triplets and sixteenth note triplets.

30

Sixteenth note triplet exercise 2

All note values

The last few pages of this book have exercises combining all of the note values and rests covered.

Here is a reminder of all of the notes and rests with their count.

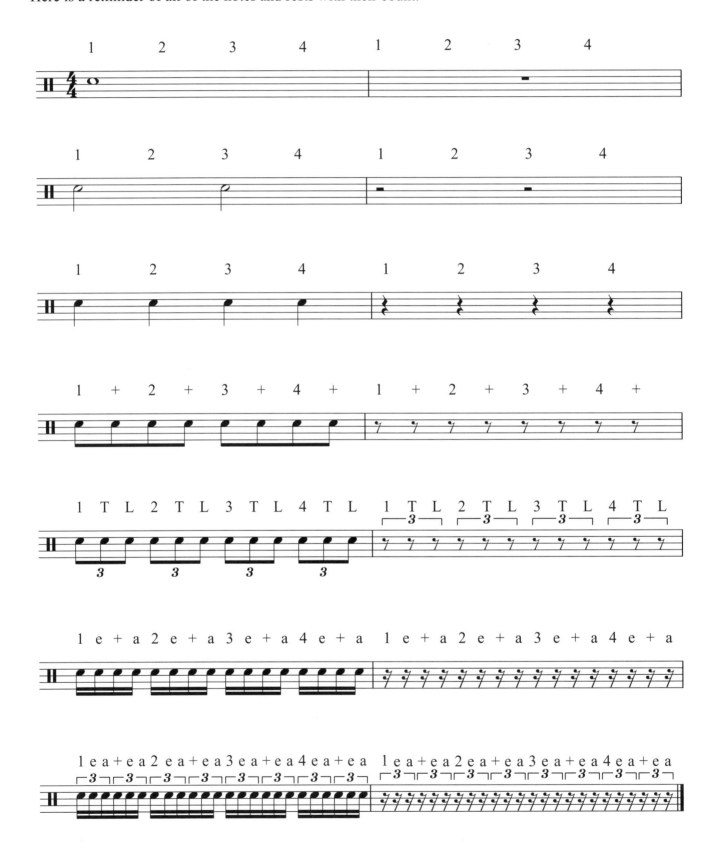

Timing exercise

This is another exercise designed to help you play all of the different note values at a constant tempo and understand their relationship to each other when playing in time.

Play each line once and then move onto the next. When you get to the bottom of the exercise, work your way back up to the top again. Repeat several times.

Play to a click, starting slowly to begin with, but experimenting with different tempos. When you find the exercise easy, mix it up by playing the different lines in a random order.

Final exercise 1

To finish off, here are two exercises combining everything covered in the book.

Final exercise 2

Final exercise 3

Final exercise 4

DRUMSENSE

What makes the Drumsense teaching programme different?
It's the approach to beginners. The approach is based on the
Drumsense books, which take the complete novice through the
basics of drum kit playing like a foundation course. It is this
programme that sets the contemporary standard for drum kit
teaching and is used by modern teachers across the country. It is
also the first programme to be aimed at both private and
peripatetic teachers (schools).

So the advantages are…?

If a drum kit student is having lessons at school from a
Drumsense programme teacher, but decides to switch to private lessons,
he or she simply looks for another Drumsense programme teacher
who will continue with the programme from where the
student left off. Similarly, if a student lives in Southampton, but
has to move to Glasgow, lessons can continue with a Drumsense
teacher in that area. If a teacher needs to take a week off without
disrupting his students' lessons, another Drumsense teacher
could fill in without any problems. Teachers could even train
their own deputies to take over in emergencies.

For more information on Drumsense visit www.drumsense.com

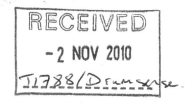